WILLIAM McCLUNG

APPALACHIAN FRONTIERSMAN

Nancy Richmond

Cover Art by Misty Murray Walkup

ACKNOWLEDGMENTS

I would like to thank my wonderful husband Charles for all the help he gave me in writing this book, which would not have been possible without his computer and editing skills and his knowledge of Greenbrier County and the Revolutionary War.

I would also like to thank my daughter Misty Murray Walkup for the original painting of William McClung that she so generously created for the cover and which now hangs over my fireplace.

Finally, I would like to thank the many descendants of William McClung (my fifth great grandfather) for all the documentation, information, and family stories they supplied, which added so much to the telling of Grandfather Billie's story.

CONTENTS

CHAPTER ONE
COLONIAL BOY

America in the seventeen hundreds was almost entirely a nation of farmers. Great Britain was the most powerful nation in the world, and had established several colonies along the eastern seaboard. France had also claimed land on the continent, and was in direct competition with England for ownership of much of the territory on the western borders of the already occupied farmlands along the coast. Living on the fringes of the wilderness often resulted in conflict between the English settlers and the French soldiers and their Native American allies.

William (Billie) McClung was born into those tumultuous times on a small farm in Rockbridge County, Virginia. The year was 1738, and Virginia was a colony of England, making the colonists subject to the British Crown and its law.

William was the third of ten children born to John and Rebecca McClung. His older brothers were Thomas and Joseph and his younger brothers were James, John, Samuel, Edward, and Charles. He had two younger sisters, Nancy and Janet.

The McClung family was of Scottish descent. William's paternal grandfather John was born in the Highlands of Scotland, near Galloway, where the McClung Clan had lived for countless generations. However, during the middle ages the conflict between the Catholics and the Protestants in that country became so violent that it was decreed that all Scots who were not Catholic were to be killed or put into prison. The only alternative for Protestants was to leave the country.

The McClung clansmen were ardent Presbyterians, so William's grandfather John immigrated with his wife and children to Ulster County, Ireland, in the late sixteen hundreds. Ulster was under British jurisdiction at that time and thousands of displaced Scottish families were permitted to move into the territory, providing they agreed to learn to speak the English language and to abide by British law.

William's father, John McClung, was born in Ireland in 1706. He traveled to the English colonies in America as a young man, like many Scottish people who were hoping to improve their situations by coming to the New World.

John settled in Pennsylvania and worked there, probably as an indentured servant, until he saved enough money to buy a 278 acre farm in the 'Forks' area of Rockbridge County, in

3

Virginia Colony. Rockbridge encompassed all of the Shenandoah Valley, which had been attracting Scotts-Irish pioneers since the early part of the century.

The Shenandoah Valley (which in the Shawnee language means 'clear eyed daughter of the stars') was first seen by English settlers when Virginian Governor Spottswood and a company of explorers gazed down on it from the peaks of the Blue Ridge Mountains in 1716. The Shawnee told the English explorers that the beauty of the Shenandoah Valley so awed the heavens that each star caste the brightest jewel from its own crown into the valley's limpid waters, there to sparkle and shine ever after in a gesture of celestial benediction.

In 1720 Benjamin Borden, an English land speculator, received a royal grant from the British giving him the authority to place one hundred families in Rockbridge County, and many Scotts-Irish immigrants quickly answered his call for homesteaders. They began to settle along a well worn Indian trail known as the Wagon Road, which ran through the center of the valley. The same general route is still used today and is known as the Valley Pike, or US Route 11.

The topography surrounding the Wagon Road was comprised mainly of meadow and savanna bottom land. It was excellent for growing grains and raising cattle, and the territory was soon dotted with farms. The name of the county, Rockbridge, was derived from 'Rocky Bridge' an early reference to the Natural Bridge of Virginia, which is one of the natural wonders of the world.

After relocating to Rockbridge, John met and married a young Scottish girl, Rebecca

Stuart, whose family were farmers in Virginia Colony. Together, the couple built a small log home and began growing corn and tobacco, the staple crops of Virginia.

John and Rebecca's children were a tremendous asset to the family, since they were needed to perform the many tasks that had to be done on the homestead. Colonial farmers who did not have children often took in orphans or youngsters whose parents could not provide for them to help with the farmwork. If no children were available and they could afford it, many farmers bought slaves as laborers.

From the age of three, William and his brothers were expected to do simple chores like feeding the chickens, stringing vegetables and gathering wild berries. Tobacco was the family's most important crop, so as he grew older William spent the largest part of each day during the summer months topping the tobacco (removing the flowers to allow the leaves to grow bigger) and picking tobacco worms off the plants. He also had to chop and carry wood on a daily basis, since fires had to be made for cooking even when the weather was warm.

Like most farmers of that time, John McClung made many of the tools that he needed on his homestead himself, as well as the simple furniture that his family used in their house. As his sons grew, they learned these skills by watching and participating whenever new items had to be made for the family. They also learned how to care for the livestock, make fences and eventually build cabins and barns.

William's sisters Nancy and Janet assisted their mother with the washing and cooking, and the making of soap and candles. They learned how to spin homespun material for summer clothing, and how to cure animal hides to make coats and boots for winter. They also learned such chores as gardening and preserving food, knitting, spinning and carding wool and child rearing.

One of the most important skills girls of that time were taught was how to use naturally growing herbs to treat illness. Additionally, the females of each family were expected to treat wounds and assist in child birth.

The McClungs, like all of the colonists of Rockbridge in the 1700s, learned from an early age to be self sufficient. Virtually everything the family had was grown or made on the farm.

Because there were no public schools in Rockbridge County at the time, Rebecca taught her children how to read and write. Nearly every pioneer household had a Bible and a 'horn book', which was a sheet of paper with the alphabet written on it that was glued to a thin rounded piece of wood. The paper was then covered by a transparent layer of animal horn to preserve it. Using these two items, most colonial children received a very rudimentary education. Boys were also taught simple math, because they were expected to keep their own family accounts when they were grown.

By the time he was fourteen, William had learned how to load and fire a muzzle loading musket and a carbine long rifle, and how to use a tomahawk. The tomahawk was one of the most necessary tools of the time. Not only was it essential for cutting brush and clearing paths, but because the guns of that time had to be reloaded between each shot, it was the second line of defense for any frontiersman after he had discharged his firearm.

Hunting, trapping and fishing were additional skills a pioneer boy had to develop in preparation for becoming a man. In the early spring months of the year, William would accompany his father and brothers into the woodlands that surrounded the farm, where he learned how to discern which animals had made the various tracks that crisscrossed the muddy soil.

William quickly understood that when he interpreted them correctly, the tracks would reveal to him the pattern of each animal's habits. But it took many hours of patient observation for William to become adept in deciphering which and how many animals (or men) had passed recently on a trail, and how to follow them.

During the hot summer months John

and his sons often walked to the nearby creek to catch fish, which were a valuable source of fresh food for the family. Any fish that were not eaten immediately could be put into barrels that were filled with salt. The salt preserved the fish for as long as six months.

Fishing poles were made from cane, hickory or maple saplings. The boys carved wooden fishing lures into the shape of minnows and stained them with berry juice to make them look natural. Hooks were fashioned by whittling down the bones of birds or small animals, and larger bones were honed down to make boning knives for filleting the fish once they were caught.

Late fall was trapping season, which not only supplied the farm with fresh meat that could be salted or hickory smoked and stored for the winter, but also provided warm furs that could be made into coats and hats. Any excess furs could be sold to supply the family with cash money, which was always scarce.

William's father had several large metal traps which had been forged by the local blacksmith. The traps worked by means of a spring which snapped shut on the leg of an unsuspecting animal.

William soon became adept at setting snares made of wire nooses that were hidden in an animal's feeding area. The snares worked well for catching muskrats, weasels and other smaller types of fur bearing animals.

Young William McClung excelled at everything he set his mind to do. He was a crack shot with a flintlock long rifle, and one of the best trappers in the area.

As he matured, William began to hear stories about the lands on the western border of the colonies, deep in the rugged Appalachian mountains, that served as a barrier between the British holdings and the French territories in the northern regions of the country.

Fur traders and explorers passing though Rockbridge told tales of forests that had never been tread by white men, with trees so large a man could hollow out a cabin inside them. They told of great herds of buffalo too numerous to be counted and of flocks of passenger pigeons so large that they would block out the sun as the flew overhead. There were thousands of miles of unclaimed land in the western Appalachians, the trappers said, and limitless opportunities for brave and determined men to make their fortune.

The more he heard of the mystcrious and bountiful wilderness on the western border, the more convinced William became that someday he would be one of the men who was willing to risk everything for the chance to carve out a new life for himself in the distant mountains.

CHAPTER TWO
WILDERNESS EXPLORER

The English colonies in America prospered and experienced a sharp increase in population due to both a high birth rate among colonists and a large number of new arrivals from Europe. Land grants from the government were no longer available, and there was no unoccupied land to be had either by immigrants or by the grown children of established farmers. Many of the ambitious young Rockbridge backwoodsmen cast a yearning gaze towards the forbidden territories that lay just beyond the western border, and William McClung was among them.

At the age of eighteen William required by law to report for duty to the British militia of Rockbridge County. The militia was an armed force composed of every free adult male citizen of the Commonwealth of Virginia capable of bearing arms. The primary purpose of the militia was to repel invasions and insurrections and to enforce the laws of the colony as set forth by British law.

The militia was often less of a fighting unit than a pool of armed men available for service on a regional basis. When problems arose, the English government put together 'marches' comprised of men from various militias to face any threat to the colonies.

When the French and Indian War began in 1754, a formal act was passed by the British Parliament further defining the rules for the Colonial militia. It read: " Whereas it is necessary, in the time of danger, that the militia should be well regulated and disciplined, and be it further enacted, by the authority of aforesaid, that every person shall be armed in the manner following, that is to say: Every soldier shall be furnished with a firelock well fixed, a bayonet fitted to the same, a double cartouch (cartridge) box, and three charges of powder, and will constantly appear with the same at the time and place appointed for muster and exercise, and shall also keep at his place of abode one pound of powder and four pounds of ball, and bring the same with him into the field when he shall be required.

And for the better training and exercising of the militia, and rendering them more serviceable, be it further enacted, that every captain shall, once in three months, and oftener if thereto required by the lieutenant or chief commanding officer in the county, muster, train and exercise his company, to be made in the months of March or April, and September or October, yearly."

The Virginia colonial militia was organized according to county, automatically making William a soldier of Rockbridge County. He and the other men in his division were on call at all times in the event of a colonial insurrection, an Indian attack, or an invasion by another country.

Because of his skill as a tracker and his reputation as a sharp shooter, William McClung was frequently chosen whenever forays onto the western border were necessary. He soon became familiar with the many mountain trails, river ways, forests and savannahs of the Appalachians, and found himself drawn to the beauty and majesty of the largely unexplored region. In the autumn William often took his rifle and tomahawk and traveled west to hunt, trap and explore along the edge of the frontier.

In 1755 a wave of settlers entered the

Greenbrier Valley without the permission of the British authorities, breaking the French Treaty of Aix-la-Chapelle, which denied English colonists the right to homestead that portion of Ohio and Virginia.

The outraged French Canadian Governor sent an an army of soldiers and Indians into the contested area, where they erected a series of lead plates with an inscription asserting French ownership of the territory. They also made treaties with many of the local Indian tribes and encouraged them to help drive the English settlers out of the valley. To further secure their rights, the French built a long line of forts along the perimeter of the disputed land to deter the English from entering the Appalachian mountains.

In retaliation, Virginia's Govenor Robert Dinwiddie instructed his militia to begin building forts to protect the English homesteaders, who had established several small camps in the areas of what are now Marlinton and Hot Springs. Before the English forts could be completed, however, bands of renegade Indians described by the colonists as 'flying parties' began terrorizing the settlements.

The war parties killed twelve settlers and captured seven more, burned their cabins and slaughtered all the livestock, leaving the settlements uninhabitable. The survivors fled across the mountains to Fort Dinwiddie, which was still under construction.

Following the massacre, there were no more attempts to settle Greenbrier County until after 1758, when British General John Forbes headed a military force that attacked the French forces at Fort Duquesne. The French were not prepared for the confrontation, and fled after blowing up the fort. With the area now under English control, the local native tribes made peace with the Crown, thus ending the danger of Indian attacks for a time.

Although the Greenbrier territory was temporarily at peace, British officials in Virginia decided not to open the area for settlement. The Greenbrier Company and several other land speculators, fearing the loss of their grants, began encouraging settlers to return to the area. They promised the homesteaders that the government would soon begin awarding land to homesteaders living in the territory. A few foolhardy colonists heeded the bad advice. In 1761 they traveled into the Lewisburg and Muddy Creek sections of Greenbrier County and set up squatters claims.

When the Ottawa tribes, led by Chief

Pontiac, learned of the settlements, they banded together with the other Indian nations to attack the homesteaders and push them back onto English occupied land. In 1763 the Shawnee Chief Cornstalk and sixty of his warriors entered the border settlement at Muddy Creek under the flag of peace. Disarmed by their seeming friendliness, the Indians were welcomed by the whites. After entering the village, the Shawnees attacked and either killed or captured all of the town's inhabitants. The natives then proceeded to the Big Levels community near Lewisburg, where they repeated their heinous atrocities.

Word of the vicious attacks reached the British government, who immediately issued an edict forbidding any English colonists to venture west of the crests of the Appalachian Mountains, and ordering any settlers who had taken up residence beyond that point to leave at once. Obeying the command, no other attempt to settle the border territories was made by the colonists.

Eventually the British army ordered Colonel Henry Bouquet to march into the wilderness with a large expedition of men negotiate peace treaties with the Mingo, Shawnee and Delaware tribes, bringing a cessation of hostilities in 1764.

For eighteen months, there were no reported confrontations between the natives and the Virginia colonists. Believing that the western borderlands would soon be legally opened for settlement, William McClung set off into the mountains to search for a tract of land on which he could eventually stake his claim.

Assuming that the ownership of the farmlands along the Greenbrier River and its immediate tributaries would be hotly contested by settlers who had lived there earlier, William chose to explore the lower portion of the county, and in 1766 he became the first white man to set foot in what is now Rupert, WV.

The grandeur of the wild and rugged landscape in the Meadow River area appealed to William's Scottish nature as well as to his love of the highland country that his father had instilled in him. He felt a kinship to the ancient forests and wild creatures that inhabited them, and was overcome by a feeling of belonging that he had never before experienced.

Although he could not make a legal claim at that time, William made up his mind to return as soon as land was opened for colonization, and make his home in the western mountains of the Greenbrier territories.

CHAPTER THREE
ABIGAIL DICKENSON

It was the custom in colonial days for the adult son of a farmer to stay with his parents and share crop the farm for a portion of the harvest, until such time as he married. The son would then build his own cabin on the farm for his family, and would eventually inherit that property when his parents passed away. That is what William and several of his brothers did when they were grown, since it was difficult to find unoccupied land in the colonies.

By the time he was twenty-eight years old, William was a respected farmer and woodsman in Rockbridge. He was very tall for a man in the seventeen hundreds, and handsome in appearance. He was considered by all to be an excellent conversationalist and an estimable citizen. The only thing that was missing was a wife with whom he could share his life, so in his typical direct fashion, he set about finding one.

The ratio of men to women in Virginia Colony was two to one, so eligible girls were rare and eagerly sought after. The rough pioneer men would gallantly court the lady of their interest, and often came to blows with other suitors who were pursuing her.

One of the most desirable girls in Rockbridge County at that time was Miss Abigail Dickenson (Carpenter). Her beauty and her spirit were well known to everyone in the area, and she had her pick of any single man in the settlement.

Abigail's parents were Joseph Carpenter and Abigail Dickenson Carpenter. Abigail was named after her mother. In colonial days girls were named for their mothers as often as boys were named for their fathers, a practice which

26

has fallen out of favor over time.

Abigail's mother died when she was only four years old. Her father could not raise the little girl on his own, so he brought Abigail back to her grandparents, Adam and Catherine Dickenson, and asked them to care for her. They agreed, and gave Abigail their surname, Dickenson, which she was known by in Rockbridge.

Abigail's father, Joseph Carpenter, was descended from some of the most noble families in Europe, and could trace his ancestry back to King William the Conqueror of England, King Alfred the Great of England, and King Charlemagne of France. Many of the younger children of royalty who did not inherit the lands and titles that were passed to the oldest son often came to America as soldiers or clergy, or to establish plantations for themselves. This was the case with the Carpenter family, who had originally settled in New York when they immigrated to America at the end of the 1600s.

So not only was Abigail young and beautiful, her Nobel background further enhanced her desirability in the eyes of the young men in Rockbridge. Additionally, her grandparents were prosperous and were held in high esteem by their neighbors, so it was no exaggeration to say that at nineteen years of age, Abigail was the undisputed belle of the county.

Since William was probably the most eligible bachelor in Rockbridge, no one was surprised when he set his sights on pretty Abigail Dickenson. Neither were they surprised when all of her other suitors decided to look elsewhere for a bride once William had declared his intentions towards Abigail, since it would not have been wise to challenge the rugged frontiersman for her favor.

Abigail soon fell in love with the handsome and engaging young backwoodsman. When William asked her to marry him after a typically short colonial courtship she readily agreed. The couple was married at the Carpenters home in Rockbridge in 1767.

William worked as a farmer on his father's land, and hunted and trapped to support himself and his new wife. They were very happy, and were well liked by the other residents of the county.

In 1768 the McClungs had their first child, a son they named John. Two years later, Abigail gave birth to their second son, James. When their third son was born the next year, he was named William but soon acquired the nickname Chunky Billie because of his stocky build and love of eating.

As the years passed, William became more and more dissatisfied with his life in Rockbridge. He often talked with Abigail about his dream of claiming a homestead in the distant Appalachians, and of the many opportunities that could be found there.

Abigail agreed that it was the only chance they would ever have to make a better life for themselves and their children. She was confident that William would be able to protect and provide for them in the wilderness. She was aware of the many dangers involved and how hard it would be to raise a family in such a hostile and uncivilized place, but like William she felt that it was worth the risks involved to be able to own their own home and to live free. Abigail promised William that she would follow him to the wilderness of Greenbrier County.

CHAPTER FOUR
TOMAHAWK ENTRY

Time passed with very few instances of conflict between the English and the French and Indians along the western border. Believing it would now be safe for British colonists to move onto the frontier, the government authorities agreed to rescind their non-settlement decree.

In January of 1768 Lord Shelburne, Secretary of State for the Southern Department and Overseer of the American Colonies for England, approved the opening of all of what is now West Virginia, southwest Virginia, and the eastern third of Kentucky for settlement.

William knew that the time had finally come for him to stake his claim on a homestead. Fearing that the best farmlands would be quickly claimed by other equally ambitious frontiersmen, William McClung said goodbye to his wife and children and set out towards the wilds of the newly available territory.

At that time there were no roads into the Appalachian Mountains, only rough paths that had been carved out by migrating buffalo herds and tribes of Indians on their summer hunting trips through the territory. There were two major trails that were traveled regularly by the Indian tribes who inhabited the eastern part of the country. The first was the Seneca Trail, which was used as a trading route between the Iroquois tribes of the north and the Cherokee tribes living in North Carolina and eastern Tennessee. The second was the Warrior Path, which intersected the Valley of Virginia, and was traversed primarily by the Shawnee and other tribes in the west.

No wagon could travel the rutted and meandering mountain byways, so the colonial frontiersmen who first pushed into the rugged forest lands used pack animals, either horses or mules, to carry their supplies.

Scores of seasoned and experienced woodsmen, William McClung among them, traveled into the uncharted and dangerous wilderness that seperated Virginia Colony and Ohio. The area consisted of over one thousand miles of largely unexplored territory that included vast forests, rugged mountains, roiling creeks and rivers, and large stretches of bottom land that would prove to be excellent for homesteading.

The Greenbrier district was riddled with limestone, which over the millennia had created numerous caves and hundreds of sinkholes where the porous soil simply dropped into yawning depressions that often extended for hundreds of feet. Great stands of primeval forest covered the surface of the mountainous regions. Red spruce, oak, maple, hickory, poplar and birch were predominant, as were the conifer white pines which were highly sought after by lumber mills as a building material.

There were large ravines that the natives called 'shades of death' because the height of the trees and the denseness of the tangled underbrush created a perpetual darkness on the valley floor that the sun never penetrated, even on the sunniest days.

The great herds of buffalo that still inhabited the Greenbrier region attracted predators such as bears, panthers and vicious packs of buffalo wolves. The buffalo wolves were much larger than other wolf species, with some weighing as much as one hundred and fifty pounds. They were very territorial and would not hesitate to attack those unfortunate souls who wandered into their hunting grounds.

The greatest danger for the hardy frontiersman, however, came from the bands of renegade Indians who frequently used the trails during their summer hunts that took them through the Appalachian forests.

Appalachia, an Indian name meaning 'endless mountains' was well suited to the land. The Appalachians are one of the oldest mountain ranges in the world, and were at one time higher in elevation than the Himalayas are today. Because of the unrelenting and foreboding nature of the mountain range with its numerous ridges and valleys, impassible swamps, dense forests and heavy underbrush, it was virtually impossible for explorers to prepare for the unexpected attacks that were frequently made by bands of rogue Indians. In the face of such obstacles, only the most resourceful and fearless frontiersmen dared to travel through the depths of the uncharted wilderness in search of a homestead.

The natives had two complaints that kept them at odds with the settlers who tried to homestead the Greenbrier and Kentucky regions. Many of the transient tribes that frequented the area believed the land was inhabited by the ghosts of an ancient tribe of white people, Azgens, who had come from an eastern sea hundreds of years earlier and had been murdered by the Shawnee tribes. The natives thought that in retaliation the ghosts of the Azgens would not allow permanent settlement on the sacred grounds, although hunting was permitted there.

In the words of the Shawnee Chief Black Fish "We are never allowed to kill the game wantonly, and we are forbidden to settle in the country. If we did, these ghosts would not rise from their caves and mounds to kill us, but they would set father against son and son against father and neighbor against neighbor and make them kill one another."

These superstitions, combined with the fear that the white settlers would deplete their hunting territory of game, often led the hunting parties to stalk and kill any small groups of white explorers that crossed their path, in spite of the treaties their chiefs had signed forbidding such hostilities.

Although he was aware of the dangers involved, William McClung did not hesitate to venture deep into the daunting wilderness. Carrying only his musket, his flintlock long rifle, his tomahawk, and the few provisions that his horses could carry, William made his way into the most rugged section of the Appalachian mountain range.

All along the Greenbrier River, adventurers began carving out settlements. The first permanent town was founded at Frankford by Colonel John Stuart, Robert McClenachan, Thomas Renick and William Hamilton. Thomas Williams took up a homestead about two miles south of what would become Williamsburg, and was soon joined by William McCoy and William Hughart. The Savanna Fort was built at Camp Union near the future site of Lewisburg, WV. Nearby, William McKinney claimed a homestead on Muddy Creek Mountain, followed by several others. John Patton established a settlement at the foot of Hughart's mountain, and William Patton took a homestead that grew into a small village on Culberton's Creek. Two recent English immigrant brothers, Jacob and Adam Mann, built a fort on Indian Creek about ten miles west of present day Union, WV. The Keeny family from the valley of Virginia also built a small fort on Keenys Knob about ten miles further south. John McNeil founded the town of Little Levels on a stream not far from what is now White Sulphur Springs, and Andrew Donnally and his family settled on the property where he would later build Fort Donnally, near present day Alta, WV.

But the land that William McClung intended to claim lay even deeper in the uninhabited parts of the county, at the top of a series of mountains that are now known as the Devil's Backbone mountain ridge, which had elevations of 2200 to 3200 feet above sea level.

William followed the dusty paths through the mountains, traveling from first light until dusk before setting up camp each evening.

He carried little in the way of supplies, instead hunting game and foraging off the abundant bounty of fruit, nuts and berries along the way.

At night William built a small fire and cooked his supper. Then, after seeing to his horses and loading his guns in case of an unexpected attack by predators or Indians, he rolled himself into his bearskin blanket and fell asleep. If he was lucky, there was sufficient underbrush or perhaps a small grotto or cave to give him protection from the elements when there was inclement weather.

The one hundred mile journey into the area of Big Clear Creek took many days, and in addition to the ever present dangers of wild animals and savages, there was a constant threat of accidents or illnesses, either of which could quickly take the life of a frontiersman along the isolated mountain trails.

At last William found himself along the banks of the river that he had explored some years earlier. Finding no indication that the land had been claimed by other explorers, McClung took a 'tomahawk entry' for one hundred thousand acres of land. A tomahawk entry was the accepted way in colonial times for a pioneer to be granted land on the frontier. Settlers would mark the corners of their homestead by ringing a tree or trees on the four corners of the claim, which would kill the trees and thus mark the land as taken. The trees would be branded with the frontiersman's mark, usually his name or initial, to differentiate the property from other claims. After the land had been occupied for a set period, the tomahawk claim could be submitted to the governing body where it would go through the legal process and be lawfully deeded to the settler.

After marking his homestead, William lingered in the wilderness only long enough to hunt fresh game to replenish his greatly reduced provisions. Then as quickly as possible he made the arduous journey back to Rockbridge to retrieve his family and begin the preparations to transport them to their new frontier home.

CHAPTER FIVE
FRONTIER FAMILY

William and Abigail were thrilled with the prospect of owning their own homestead. They spent the last few weeks of winter making plans for their journey into the frontier. William told the children stories of the many wonderful things he had seen on his trip through the wilderness, and they were as excited as their parents to become pioneers in the Greenbrier territory.

As soon as spring rains of 1770 melted the snow from the Indian trails in the newly available territory, hundreds of settlers poured onto the western borders of Virginia in search of homesteads.

To acquire legal rights to his tomahawk entry, William was required to move onto the claim with his family and homestead the land for one year. They needed to make the move in time to plant a spring crop, or else they would risk starvation during the coming winter. So he and Abigail settled their accounts in Rockbridge and sold anything that could not be taken with them to their new home in Appalachia.

They bought or traded for black powder and the lead they would need for making bullets. They also bought seed corn, rope, sugar, salt and other items that would not be available in the wilderness. Other than personal items, the only necessities that they packed for the journey were an ax and shovel, oil lamps, a large wash tub for bathing and for washing clothes, and a cast iron cooking pot.

William and Abigail said farewell to their family and friends, not knowing if they would ever see them again. Then, loading as much as they could manage onto their pack horses, which were tethered together single file, they set off with their three young children into the unknown.

There would be no doctors or even friendly settlers along the long, lonely stretches of Indian trail they had to follow, and the risks they faced were made greater by the isolation of the new territory. The young couple would be responsible for hunting, growing or making everything the little pioneer family would need to survive.

The trip that had taken weeks for William to complete the previous year was made even longer by the slow pace they set in order to care for the needs of three small children. The family was amazed by the huge trees, some as large as eight feet in diameter, that bordered the well worn path. There was an abundance of wild life that had no fear of the pioneers, sometimes walking out of the forest to stand silently watching as they passed by.

When the Indian trail they were traveling veered away from the direction of their homestead, William had to use his ax to clear an opening wide enough for the horses to pass though as they continued their journey, which slowed their progress considerably. Higher and higher into the rugged mountains they traveled, until they could no longer see the valley floor below them.

It took several days from the time the McClungs left the Indian trail until they finally reached the edge of the property that bore the distinctive markings of William's tomahawk entry. Now the couple had to pick a good location for their new home.

Eventually a large meadow with a meandering river bordering one side opened before them. In later years the meadow would come to be known as McClung Meadow, and the river that ran through it became the Meadow River, which is still its name today. It was a beautiful spot, but William was sure that the low lying meadow would flood when the snow from the nearby mountains melted each spring, which made it a poor choice for a homestead.

The family traveled on and at length made camp on a ridge overlooking a crystal clear creek. An ancient pine tree stood majestically on the ridge, its huge branches spreading their shade onto the water below. William named the place Pine Ridge, and it was there that the pioneers built the little one room cabin that would be their home for the next three years. The site was about one mile from the present day town of Rupert, on what is now

Tommy Hall Road.

The weary travelers unloaded their belongings and made camp for the last time, happy that they had finally reached their homestead. The next morning William began cutting logs from which to create a 'half-faced camp', which was a rough shelter made by stacking logs on three sides and covering the top with pliable tree limbs that served as a partial roof and afforded some protection from the weather.

While Abigail moved the children and their supplies into the relative safety of the temporary structure, William began marking off the perimeters for the one room cabin he planned to build. After considering several large pine trees, he selected one that measured some six feet in diameter. He felled the tree and cut it in half. Using his ax blade, William flattened and smoothed both sides of each piece and tied them together with a length of rope, making a sled that he harnessed to his horses. He then led his team down the steep ravine to the edge of the nearby creek. From the bottom of the stream William selected four large smooth stones to be used as his home's foundation. Loading them on his makeshift sled, he returned to the campsite and laid the river rocks in the sun to dry.

The next day, after setting the stones in the soft soil that he had loosened with his ax, William began felling the trees that he would use as the walls of the cabin, which would measure sixteen feet long and ten feet wide. William dug out shallow trenches between the corner stones, then picked four sturdy pines to be the support beams of the house. He rolled the first two sixteen foot logs into their trenches, then cut deep grooves at the end of each, where the ten foot sections would be connected.

Round and round the walls he went, rolling trees into their notched sections, until the cabin stood as high as he could reach. Abigail and the children helped by filling the spaces between the logs with small stones, twigs, and moss. Then they plastered the holes with a mixture of ground limestone and mud, making a tight seal that no wind or rain could penetrate.

William cut the last few logs shorter than the others, and with them he formed a peak at the end of each of the ten foot sections. Between these he placed a center post and attached slender poles across the frame to form the roof. Cutting small squares of bark into workable pieces that resembled shingles,

William created a rough covering for the poles, using mud and small pegs that he had whittled to fasten them together. The shingles overlapped one another to prevent leaks.

William next cut out openings for a door and for two windows, one on each side of the cabin. Since they did not have glass for the windows, he built wooden shutters that could be opened during the day to let in light and closed at night or during bad weather.

For the door, William cut a heavy four foot by six foot wood slab, which he rubbed with an oil cloth until it was smooth. The door was fastened to the house using pegs, and fitted with a string latch that acted as a door knob and could be pulled in at night to secure the cabin.

Finally, William built a stone fireplace using rocks from the stream and crushed limestone mixed with mud. In only three days

William had built a cozy home for his family, without using even one nail.

Once the cabin was finished, William set about making two bedsteads, a large one for himself and Abigail, and a smaller one for the boys that could be pushed under the big bed during the day. Abigail sewed two large bags from animal hides that she filled with fresh grass for use as mattresses on the rough hewn beds.

Will next built a table using two logs as legs and a smoothed slab for a top. For chairs, the family used tree stumps whose tops were polished down so they would not have splinters. While William worked, Abigail wove several large baskets using reeds from the nearby swamp to hold the family's clothing and other belongings. Then William drove two large pegs into the wood above the door on which to hang his rifle, so that he could reach it quickly if he needed it.

In the days that followed, William built a shelter for the livestock. He encircled it with a rustic split rail fence, and the little pioneer farm was complete.

After hunting for meat to replenish the family's dwindling food supplies, William's next task was to clear a tract of land of trees so that he could plant the seeds that they had brought with them on the journey west.

Smaller trees could be cut down, but the larger ones had to be killed first by 'girdling' them, which was done by removing a strip of bark completely around the circumference of the tree. After the trees died and dried out, they could be cut down and used as firewood.

Because they had only been able to bring the most necessary items with them to the wilderness on their packhorses, William made many of the tools he needed on the farm after he reached his homestead. Most were cut and carved out of wood, including his hoe, rake and plow.

William's plow was a simple device that had been invented in the mid 1700s and had become very popular in the English colonies. Called a shovel plow, it was simply a wide and shallow piece of wood resembling a shovel that was attached to a long pole. The pole had a hole bored through one end. A sturdy rope was threaded through the hole and attached to the traces of a horse, which pulled the plow through the field. The primitive but effective plow broke up the soil so that the seeds could be buried in the loose dirt.

By the time the spring planting season arrived, William had cleared off a large section of bottom land below the ridge where the cabin stood. The fields were bordered by the creek on one side and a large dismal swamp on the other. William took supplies for the day and left Abigail and their three small sons at the cabin whenever the fields needed to be tended, returning home at dusk.

Every evening, after the chores were done, William carved spoons, bowls and plates for the family. He also made pails and barrels for carrying water and storing food, and wall shelves to hold their lanterns and his gunpowder and other hunting supplies.

The McClung farm stood absolutely alone within the vast forest. There were no other homes, stores, or villages for many miles in any direction. In late autumn, William made a two day trip to Matthews Trading Post on the Greenbrier River, where he exchanged the furs he had trapped that summer for sugar, salt, lamp oil and the other supplies they would need until spring.

The first long winter that the pioneer family spent in the Appalachian wilderness was harsher than any they had ever experienced in the gently rolling hills of Rockbridge County.

As early as October the snow began to fall, often drifting as high as the shuttered windows. The frigid winds howled, freezing the creek and making it almost impossible to leave the warmth of the cabin. But the land had provided them with an abundance of food and animal furs, and the long winter months were spent securely in the safety of their snug mountain home, even when panthers screamed in the nearby forest and the hungry buffalo wolves howled outside the heavy wooden door.

William spent the chilly grey days making bullets and smoothing wood to make buckets for collecting sap from the nearby maple trees in the spring, so that they could make maple syrup. He went outside only to bring in wood to keep the hearth fire blazing, and in the morning and evening to tend to the horses.

Abigail sewed warm and waterproof buckskin garments and boots for William to wear while he hunted and trapped during the winter months. She attached long fringes of leather to the sleeves and legs of the buckskins, to help camouflage William from Indians or predators whenever he traveled through the forest. She sewed smaller versions of the buckskins that William wore for her three boys. She also tanned the furs from the smaller animals that had been trapped that fall, so that they could been sewn together into warm blankets and rugs for the hard dirt floor of their log cabin home.

James, John and Chunky Billie stayed busy helping their parents with any chores that they were big enough to do. In the evenings they played by the fire with the wooden toys that William whittled for them and listened to the stories that their mother read to them from their family Bible.

The McClungs, happy and contented on their homestead, had no way of knowing that their new life would soon be shattered by war.

CHAPTER SIX
INDIAN UPRISING

Like the McClung family, most of the pioneers living on the western border believed that they no longer had anything to fear from the Indians who used the area as a hunting territory.

But in spite of the treaties that had been made between the English and the numerous Indian tribes that roamed the western borders of the colonies, many of the natives were angry because the Virginian authorities did not honor their agreement to keep settlers out of the lands south of the Ohio River. The Shawnees began recruiting other tribes to attack the invading homesteaders, and were soon joined by renegade bands of warriors from the Mingo, Cherokee, Wyandotte, Delaware, Miami and Wabash nations.

Early in 1773 hostilities between the Indians and the colonists were resumed when a band of Shawnee warriors murdered George Yeager, a farmer whose homestead lay along the banks of the Elk River. Soon after, a group of settlers traveling to Kentucky under the leadership of Daniel Boone were waylaid and five people were killed, including Boone's son. The remaining survivors retreated back to the east.

Word of the recent insurrections had not reached William McClung on his isolated homestead, but he had seen signs that Indians were crossing his claim in increasing numbers. Smoke from their campfires and sometimes the sounds of their passing could be heard from the little cabin on the ridge.

The roving bands of savages had become so common that William feared leaving

Abigail and the children alone when it came time for him to do his spring plowing. Rather than risk them being attacked while he was away, he built a small shelter in the swamp near his fields. William then camouflaged the hut with moss so that it could not be easily seen by passing renegades.

Abigail and the boys accompanied William to the bottom lands and spent the day hiding in the swamp while he worked, then they returned to the cabin together in the evening.

William loaded his musket and gave it to Abigail to protect the children, while he carried his long rifle over his shoulder as he worked his fields. He remained within easy earshot of the swamp, so he could come to the defense of his family at a moment's notice if necessary.

The McClungs spent an undisturbed summer on their farm, but eventually William knew the danger from the marauding savages was too great, and when Abigail told him she was expecting another child he knew they could not stay on the homestead. With a heavy heart William loaded the horses with as much as they could carry, and with his family made the long journey through the wilderness to Williamsburg, which was the closest settlement to the McClung claim.

Williamsburg was situated near one of the English stockades that had been built the year before, which lessened the chance of an Indian attack. William knew they would not be able to return to their homestead until peace was made between the Indians and the English government. He and his family found shelter with the inhabitants of the town, whose citizens were glad to welcome refugees from the neighboring border, since it added able bodied men to their ranks in case of an Indian uprising.

By 1774 most of the western tribes were in open rebellion against the settlers. Unlike the more organized Indian attacks that had been under the control of the French in the past, small bands of renegades traveled through the Greenbrier Valley at will, assaulting any homesteaders they came across, killing and scalping men, women, and children and burning their homes.

One raiding party attacked a small settlement at Cedar Grove, killing homesteader Walter Kelly and his young servant boy. The remainder of the inhabitants managed to escape to safety, but the village was lost.

Infuriated, the frontiersmen began making raids of their own into Indian territory. Not knowing which natives were making attacks against the settlements, they sometimes killed the members of friendly tribes, further inflaming the hostilities.

That summer Indians attacked a group of militia under Captain John Dickinson at the mouth of the Greenbrier River. Several militiamen were wounded and one was killed. Around the same time, Arbuckle's Fort at Muddy Creek was fired on, and in July one of the survivors of the Cedar Grove massacre (Walter Kelly's brother) was killed just outside the fort. His young daughter, who was with him at the time, was carried off by the raiding party.

As a result of the atrocities, the government authorities in charge of the border ordered a series of forts to be built along the edge of the colonial settlements, to give homesteaders a safe retreat in the case of an Indian assault. Soon a line of small stockades dotted the landscape, affording the settlers at least a modicum of safety from the hostile tribes.

In the fall of 1774 the British authorities issued a letter of warning to the colonial militia, telling them to expect an imminent attack by the natives, and to be prepared to repel their advance.

William McClung and the other border men prepared for the approaching battle, and were eager to repay the Indians for the outrages of the previous year. The angry backwoodsmen took the letter to be a declaration of war, and dubbed the conflict 'Cresaps War' in memory of a group of surveyors led by Michael Cresap that had been attacked by a war party that spring.

A company of frontiersmen raided several Indian encampments, including the village of a friendly group of Mingo tribesmen, where they killed the family of Chief Logan. Their actions further inflamed the anger of the local natives towards the settlers.

Lord Dunmore, governor of the territory, directed Colonel Andrew Lewis to build a fort on the Kanawha River as a base of operations and then to destroy all the Indian villages in the area. Lewis immediately complied.

At the same time Major Angus McDonald led an army of four hundred soldiers from Fort Dunmore to the Shawnee village of Wakotomica on the Muskingum River, hoping to make a treaty with their Chief. However, Indian scouts warned the natives of the approaching soldiers, and the village was deserted when the army arrived. In anger, the Major ordered that the town be burned to the ground, then he returned with his men to the Shenandoah Valley.

Learning of McDonald's failure, Lord Dunmore called for the creation of a large expeditionary force to combat the Indian threat. Dunmore himself headed a British army regiment of thirteen hundred men. Colonel Andrew Lewis was named commander of the combined regular army forces and the militia from the southern territories.

The call to arms was answered by hundreds of frontiersman from the border, all anxious to free the area from the Indian menace. William McClung was among the group of Greenbrier militiamen who gathered at the Barracks, a military garrison that had been built in 1770 at what is now Lewisburg, West Virginia.

Many years later President Theodore

Roosevelt, when studying the history of the
upcoming battle, stated that "It may be doubted
if ever a braver or physically finer set of men
were ever got together on this continent."

Although they did not have standard
uniforms like the army regulars, the seasoned
frontiersmen were more or less equally garbed
in the traditional hunting gear of the day, which
included buckskin shirts and leggings and
animal skin caps. Every man wore a pair of
deerskin boots that came almost to the knees, in
order to protect them from rattlesnake and
copperhead bites in the snake infested forests.

The border men carried either muskets or
flintlock rifles, tomahawks, knives, and horns of
black powder. Most of the men were excellent
marksmen and were unparalleled trackers.
Altogether, the soldiers of the colonial militia
were a fearsome and intimidating force to be

reckoned with.

Dunmore sent a post to Colonel Lewis instructing him to march his men down the Kanawha and rendevous with the regular army there. The troops set out on the eighth of September, with a band of men numbering eleven hundred. Their one hundred and sixty mile route had been charted by Captain Mathew Arbuckle, an able bodied scout who knew the territory well.

The army made slow progress, for there were no trails wide enough to accommodate such a large brigade of men with its supply train of wagons, pack horses, and cattle. A core of experienced ax men fronted the expedition, chopping trees and widening paths so that the army could pass through the heavily forested wilderness.

Arbuckle's route led the colonial forces

over Muddy Creek Mountain, Meadow Creek, Walkers Creek and Buffalo Branch before turning northwest towards what is now Ansted. Much of the land was unexplored territory for the Englishmen.

Even seasoned woodsmen like William McClung were awed by the depths of the dark and gloomy forests which did not even have animal trails for the convoy to follow, and by the rocky and nearly impassable mountains they had to navigate on the long march towards the head of the Kanawha River.

The army reached its destination at the mouth of Elk Creek, where the community of Charleston is now located, a week later. Here they made camp and built several large canoes to transport their supplies down the river.

The militia divided, with some of the men traveling by boat while the rest marched along the Indian trail that skirted the base of the mountain. After a four day inland march, they reunited at what is now Point Pleasant, where Colonel Lewis expected to join with Dunmore's army.

Several days later, however, one of Dunmore's scouts brought Lewis a message, which informed him that the Governor and his men had already crossed the river and built a fort at the mouth of the Hocking River. The message also stated that Dunmore was on route to the Pickaway plains and instructed Lewis to meet with him there. Lewis communicated the information to his captains, and they agreed to leave the following morning in accordance with Dunmore's orders.

William McClung and the other footsore frontiersmen banked their campfires and settled down for the night, knowing they faced a long march the following day. However, just before dawn, Shawnee Chief Cornstalk and over one thousand warriors who had been following the army at a distance surrounded the camp. Cornstalk's scouts had been monitoring the progress of Lewis and his troops since they left Fort Union weeks earlier, and now their Chief made the decision to attack the militia before they had time to unite their forces with those of the regular army under Dunmore's command.

In what was a stroke of luck for the Virginians, several men left the camp just before dawn to go hunting for deer. Upon entering a meadow they saw before them an uncountable number of Indian braves, covering about five acres of land. The Indians opened fire but one man managed to elude the savages and make it back in time to alert the camp of the pending attack.

The militia drums began to beat, sounding the alarm for the soldiers to prepare for battle. William and his fellow frontiersmen loaded their weapons and awaited orders from the commanding officers.

When the Indians charged, two groups of about one hundred and fifty men rushed to the forefront of the troops to meet the attack, with the frontier militiamen leading the way. The fight took place over a one mile front, with each side within plain sight of one another at all times. The militia pressed ever forward, and the Indian braves began to retreat. The desperate confrontation lasted until well past noon, when the savages took cover in the forest and disappeared into the trees, carrying their dead and wounded with them. Sporadic firing continued from each side until about eleven o'clock that night, and after that only the moaning of the wounded from both sides could be heard.

When the battle of Point Pleasant ended, the militia casualties numbered almost one fifth of their forces, and the Shawnee deaths were reported to be much higher. Many men from the McClung family fought with the Rockbridge militia, and William McClung's older brother Thomas was among those killed. William was not injured during the conflict, and like the other frontiersmen who were still able to fight, was eager to follow the Indians into the forest and continue the battle.

Colonel Lewis sent a dispatch to Governor Dunmore with details of the Battle of Point Pleasant. Two days later an answer arrived, ordering Lewis to meet Dunmore in Chillicothe so that they could join forces and pursue the renegades together.

Leaving the camp and the wounded soldiers under the command of one of his officers, Lewis and the men who could still fight headed off to meet Dunmore and the regular army. The frontiersmen were in good humor and determined to destroy the entire Shawnee nation if given the chance.

Dunmore and his troops were several days march ahead of Lewis and his band of backwoodsmen, and before the two armies could merge, Dunmore was met by Chief Cornstalk and a group of leaders from the other tribes who were anxious to sue for peace.

Dunmore and his men set up a temporary headquarters, Camp Charlotte, where he could treat with the Indians. He sent word to Colonel Lewis to leave his slow moving army and come at once to the negotiations, but the frontiersmen were so bent on attacking the Indians again that

Lewis decided against leaving them, for fear that they might initiate another battle in his absence.

The Indians, worried that the militia men would attack the villages that lay between them and Camp Charlotte, positioned braves along the river bank at they passed by, and it was only with great difficulty that Lewis was able to restrain the angry militiamen from firing on them.

Even after they reached Dunmore's camp, Lewis had to set triple guards around the perimeter of his backwoods troops to ensure that they did not kill both Governor Dunmore and the Indian Chiefs.

On the twentieth of October, the Treaty of Camp Charlotte was signed. The terms of the agreement stated that the Indian tribes involved in the insurrection would no longer hunt in the territories that are now West Virginia and

Kentucky, and that they would return any captives and horses that had been taken during the raids of the past two years. Each of the Chiefs had to agree to turn over members of their tribes to be held as hostages by Dunmore, as proof of their sincerity in keeping the treaty.

Many of the frontier militiamen were not happy with the treaty and argued that they should be allowed to exterminate any Indians still on Virginia soil, and it took much persuasion on the part of Colonel Lewis to finally convince the men to make the one 160 mile journey back to the Virginia settlements. Eventually they agreed, and William McClung was able to return to Williamsburg where Abigail and his sons were anxiously waiting for news of the expedition.

As insurance that the Indians would adhere to the dictates of the treaty, Dunmore commissioned the army to build a fort at Point

Pleasant, and left a garrison of seventy five men to intercept any war parties that might attempt to return to Virginia from the Ohio shore. The resulting outpost was named Fort Blair. The stockade was eighty feet in length and had two blockhouses to shelter the troops, making it one of the largest forts on the border. It became the first line of defense between the settlers in the Greenbrier territory and the Indian tribes of Ohio.

The defeat of the Shawnee tribe at Point Pleasant was so debilitating that all of the western Indian tribes maintained peaceful relations with the homesteaders until after the outbreak of the Revolutionary War in 1775.

CHAPTER SEVEN
CAPTAIN BILLIE

The victory at Point Pleasant brought a new feeling of confidence to the pioneers living in Greenbrier County. After the signing of the Treaty of Camp Charlotte, the Indian menace in western Virginia was greatly diminished. New homesteaders began moving into the area, and those who had left returned.

The McClungs welcomed a fourth child, a daughter that they named Catherine after the grandmother who had raised Abigail, while they were living in Williamsburg. They were thrilled to have a daughter at last, and eagerly awaited spring so that they could return to their farm and resume their lives.

In April, the family made the twenty mile journey back to their farm. They decided to build a new cabin that would be near a little spring, giving them easy access to fresh water. Their second home was closer to the fields that William farmed, making it simpler for him to keep a watchful eye on his family in case of trouble. It was also larger, with a family room, a bedroom, and a loft where the children slept. The cabin stood only a few hundred yards from a well worn path called the Buffalo Trail, that traveled along the Meadow River through what is now Rainelle and around the Little Sewell Mountain. The route would later be known as the Midland Trail, and eventually became the James River and Kanawha Turnpike.

William's sons, John, James and Chunky Billie were now big enough to help with the many tasks that were part of every farmer's life. William also began teaching them to fish and track game.

Several new homesteads were claimed

along the Meadow River, making the area less isolated, and the settlers living along the western border of the Virginia Colony experienced a short time of peace. Five of William's brothers followed him to Greenbrier County. John and James claimed land along Big Clear Creek, near William's farm. James' wife Nancy had been captured by Indians when she was only a few months old. She was returned to a fort as a young child during a prisoner exchange, but since her parents were not known, she was adopted by Col. Dickerson and took his name. She and James had been married only a short time before moving to the border.

William's younger brothers Samuel and Edward took homesteads on Muddy Creek Mountain. Samuel was well known on the frontier as an Indian fighter. In one incident a large party of braves chased him until he came to a wide ravine. He could not climb down the steep rocks, so instead he made a seemingly impossible jump to the other side of the cliff that won him the respect and admiration of the pursuing Indians.

William's youngest brother Charles also immigrated to the border and became friends with several of the local Indian tribes, whom he sometimes lived with. On several occasions he was called upon to serve as a mediator between the pioneers and the natives, and he often acted as a scout for the militia. Charles, who never married, was later one of the first settlers in what is now Charleston, WV. He was appointed as Justice of the Peace for Kanawha County by the Governor, and was the clerk at the first court ever held in Kanawha County, which appointed Daniel Boone to be the Lieutenant Colonel of the district.

The security that the settlers had been enjoying came to and end, however, when in the spring of 1775 the American colonists rebelled against England. The fragile peace along the frontier was broken, and Virginia Colony and the homesteaders along the western border quickly became embroiled in the conflict.

The Revolutionary War erupted because many of the colonists of the English provinces had become disillusioned with British rule. They believed that they did not receive any benefits from their home country, only taxes and little representation. The colonists became further inflamed by the English Proclamation of 1763, which forbade any settlement beyond the Appalachian Mountains; by the Currency Act of 1764, which banned the colonies from printing their own money; and by the Quartering Act of 1765, which forced colonists to house and feed

British soldiers without reimbursement by the English government.

By 1775 each of the colonies had established its own Provincial Congress, even though they agreed that they were still a part of the British Crown. In response to the colonist's attempts to govern themselves, the King sent combat troops to America to re-impose direct English rule over the country.

Although some colonists (known as loyalists) did not rebel against the Crown, William McClung and most of the other settlers on the border felt deeply that the people of America had the right to govern themselves, and were willing to fight for their freedom from what they perceived to be tyranny on the part of England.

When the rebellion broke out Governor Dunmore, who had been instrumental in achieving peace with the Shawnee tribes, declared himself to be a staunch loyalist. He induced the Indians to help England subdue the rebellious colonists, once more stirring up the animosity on the border that had briefly been squelched.

Dunmore also ordered that all the troops occupying Fort Dunmore, Fort Fincastle and Fort Blair be sent home and that the forts be abandoned. These actions left the Greenbrier district virtually defenseless in case of an attack from Indians or from the British army. Angry colonists forced Dunmore to flee the country, and established the Virginia Convention to take over the government of Virginia Colony.

When the anxious homesteaders along the border asked for help from the newly formed government, the Convention sent Captain John Neville of the Revolutionary Forces with one hundred soldiers to occupy Fort Pitt. Before they could send troops to Fort Blair, however, the Shawnee burned the abandoned fort to the ground.

Seeking to avert any further hostilities, the Virginia Convention sent an envoy to treat with the leaders of the western tribes, hoping to make them allies of the rebel colonists. In September of 1755 Thomas Walker, Andrew Lewis, James Wood, James Walker and Adam Stephen signed a treaty with the chiefs of the Shawnee, Delaware, Mingo, Seneca, Wyandotte, Pottawatomi, and Ottawa tribes. The agreement set the Ohio River as the southern border of the land belonging to the Indians. The natives also agreed to remain neutral in the event of any battles that took place between the English and the Americans.

After the atrocities of the previous years,

however, many of the homesteaders did not trust the Indians to honor the agreement, and a series of small, privately owned forts sprang up in the region.

Fort Arbuckle was built at the mouth of Mill Creek by the Arbuckle family who owned the land. Andrew Donnally erected a small stockade around ten miles northwest of Lewisburg. Settlers at Fort Spring collaborated to build Fort Stuart and Mann's Fort was built ten miles west of present day Union. The fears of the settlers were well founded, because by the spring of 1776 American scouts reported signs that the Indian tribes were preparing for war.

In answer to pleas for protection from the homesteaders, the Continental Congress agreed to pay the expenses of the garrisons at Fort Randolph and Point Pleasant. In addition, Governor Patrick Henry also deployed one hundred men from the newly formed American militia to be stationed at each.

Still, Fort Randolph was more than one hundred miles from the Greenbrier area and afforded little protection from small bands of roving Indians, who could attack settlers and then vanish back into the forest long before help could arrive from so far away.

John Stuart wrote to the Botetourt County commander, Colonel William Fleming, alerting him to the peril of the settlers on the border. Stuart requested that three companies of militiamen be assigned to the area, one at Muddy Creek, one at Indian Creek and one at the Levels.

Realizing the precarious position of the homesteaders, Fleming sent some of his own men as well as men from the unit of Captain Samuel Brown to build a new fort at Camp

Union. He also promised to send more militia and a large amount of gun powder to defend the fort as soon as possible.

Encouraged by his success, Stuart asked Fleming to garrison additional men at Fort Donnally and at Muddy Creek. Fleming answered regretfully that he could not spare any more of the militia unless an actual attack was made against the settlers.

Fleming put Captain George Givens in charge of the men sent to defend the Greenbrier Valley. Givens sent fifteen men to Fort Bibber on Wolf's Creek, and another fifteen to Fort Donnally. The remainder of the company were garrisoned at the new fort at Camp Union.

Believing that they were in no immediate danger from the western tribes and being further bolstered by the knowledge that there were nearby forts with garrisons of trained soldiers keeping watch over the area, William McClung decided to stay on his farm, although he kept a sharp watch for any signs of aggression by the local natives.

William was one of the first men in the county to sign the Virginia Oath of Allegiance, which the Continental Congress required from all of its adult male citizens in order to determine the strength of the patriot movement and to identify loyalists. Traveling to the nearest justice of the peace, William solemnly repeated the Oath of Virginia, saying "I do swear that I renounce and refuse all allegiance to George the Third, King of Great Britain, his heirs and successors, and that I will be faithful and bear true allegiance to the Commonwealth of Virginia, as a free and independent state, and that I will not, at any time, do, or cause to be done, any matter or thing that will be prejudicial or injurious to the freedom and independence thereof, as declared by Congress; and also, that I will discover and make known to some one justice of the peace for the said state, all treasons or traitorous conspiracies which I now or hereafter shall know to be formed against this or any of the United States of America". By taking the oath, William knew he was guilty of treason against England and was subject to death by hanging if the British won the war, but that did not deter him.

Now thirty eight years old, William was a respected and trusted man on the frontier. He had the reputation of being a deadly shot with his rifle, and of keeping a cool head during a fight. Along with most of the other Greenbrier men, William joined the American militia, which had been created by the Third Virginia Convention. The Convention had passed an ordinance for raising and embodying a sufficient

91

force for the defense and protection of Virginia. The ordinance divided Virginia into fifteen districts, each of which was to raise one company of sixty-eight men who would be a part of two regular regiments. In addition, each district was to create a battalion of minutemen who were to receive twenty days of immediate training and twelve days of training twice each year thereafter. The rest of the men of the district were to be members of the militia, which was to muster at least eleven times year and be available for short term drafts if needed to protect the newly formed country.

Because of his abilities as a rifleman and a tracker, William was promoted to the rank of ensign in the militia, which is a position similar to that of a captain in the armed forces today.

The men under William's command had a great admiration for him. He was a capable leader and a good friend to his soldiers, who often referred to him as 'Captain Billie'. The nickname became popular with the both the army regulars and the backwoods militiamen, and William continued to be called Captain Billie by many of his acquaintances, even after the war had ended.

Although the rebellion was creating havoc in the coastal colonies, British regular soldiers did not advance as far as the western borders of Virginia. The Indians, for the time being at least, had not broken their treaties. The fall and winter of 1776 passed without any real threats to the homesteaders, as did the early spring of 1777.

William began breaking the soil and plowing his fields in preparation for the spring planting, assisted by his two older sons. He had seen no sign of Indian tracks around his cabin and had not heard of any raids on nearby settlements, so he and Abigail hoped that the war would not invade the settlements along the Meadow River and Big Clear Creek.

Unfortunately, the plans that the British were formulating ensured that the entire Greenbrier Valley would soon be at the center of three large expeditions being sent against the American forces in the east. The British commander in Detroit, Henry Hamilton, had been ordered to meet with the nearby Indian tribes and make them allies to the Crown. The natives agreed and promised Hamilton at least one thousand warriors that would be ready to attack the Virginia borders on his command.

Late in July Chief Cornstalk's sister Nonhelema arrived at Fort Randolph and asked to speak with Matthew Arbuckle. Nonhelema, a Christian, had always been a friend to the white settlers, and she warned Arbuckle that there were war parties on the way to attack the Greenbrier homesteaders.

Arbuckle send out word to the nearby forts, urging them to prepare for war. It was not long until the Indians struck.

On the first of September, the combined forces of the Shawnee and other western tribes attacked Fort Henry. Twenty-five settlers were killed on the first day of the battle, and twenty-five houses were burned. The Indians destroyed all the horses and cattle on the nearby farms, and the few survivors of the attack were left without any food or shelter.

The warring tribes continued southward into Greenbrier County, and just before dawn on the eleventh of September a large war party attacked Van Bibber's Fort and several cabins standing just beyond its walls. During the raid three men were killed and a young girl, Elizabeth Graham, was taken hostage. She eventually was adopted by Chief Cornstalk and his family and remained with her captors until 1785, when she was ransomed and returned to her home.

The Indians split into several large divisions, attacking people and settlements whenever they came upon them. Most of the homesteaders fled to the forts for protection, leaving their homes to be burnt by the marauding Indians.

Two details of scouts that had been sent out by the militia engaged in battle with the warring braves during the fall. On one occasion two men were killed and on the other twenty one men were massacred, including the leader of the expedition, Captain William Foreman.

Several years earlier, the Shawnee Chief Cornstalk had been made the leader of a confederacy of Indian tribes, and it had been his decision that all the tribes would make peace with the settlers at the end of the French and Indian wars. Fearing reprisals by the whites on all the tribes because of the new hostilities, Cornstalk and two other Chiefs, Red Hawk and Petalla, journeyed to Fort Randolph in an effort to make a new peace treaty.

When they arrived at the stockade and asked to treat with the leader of the fort, the commander mistakenly thought the Indians were involved in a plot to deceive him, and took them prisoner. A few weeks later Cornstalk's son Elinipsico made his way to the fort looking for his father and was arrested also.

On the tenth of November, two boys from the fort rowed a canoe across the river to hunt deer. A nearby raiding party spotted the boys as they were returning to the river and opened fire on them. The boys ran back into the woods, shouting for help.

Several men from the fort leaped into a canoe that was tied up on the bank, and rowed across the river to rescue the boys. One young man was unharmed, but they found the second boy lying dead in the forest. He had been shot and scalped, and was covered in blood from the many wounds the Indians had inflicted on him.

Enraged, the frontiersmen returned to the fort and demanded that Cornstalk and the other prisoners be executed. Against the wishes of the fort commander, the angry mob dragged the captives from their cell and killed them.

The authorities, believing that the deaths of the hostages would bring about open warfare between the whites and the natives, held trials for the four men who were instrumental in the murders. However, because of the lack of witnesses, the men were acquitted of all the charges and released.

When William McClung heard the outcome of the proceedings, he began preparing for the retaliation of the Indians which he knew would soon follow. With no other settlers within miles of their homestead, William was the only protection that his wife and children had while they were living outside the fort.

Knowing they would have only a short time to reach the safety of nearby Fort Donnally in the case of an attack, William kept a his rifle and musket loaded at all times, and placed a pack of provisions in a bag beside the door so that the family could flee at a moment's notice.

Over the following weeks, William began marking a carefully planned trail through the woods that would take his family directly to the fort in case of an Indian raid. The escape route would be relatively easy to follow, even in the case of a night attack, but would keep them out of sight of any raiding parties passing through the area.

Then, sure that he had done everything he could to prepare for the inevitable attack, William hung his rifle over the door of the cabin — and waited.

CHAPTER EIGHT
FORT DONNALLY ATTACK

William McClung increased the frequency of the militia meetings with his men during the early months of the winter, hoping to prepare them for the hostilities he knew were sure to come. But the single digit temperatures, icy winds and enormous snowdrifts that yearly rendered the Appalachian roadways nearly impassable from November until March prevented an organized strike by the Indian tribes during the final months of 1777, and the Greenbrier residents spent a quiet if uneasy winter on their homesteads.

On December 20, Abigail presented William with another son, whom they named Joseph. He was the first white child ever born in the Meadow Bluff district.

Eventually the heavy snowfalls changed

into to warm rains and spring returned to the Appalachians. As the soft ground dried and the trees began to bloom, the English set their plans into motion.

William began to see signs that a few small bands of Indians had passed through the forest near his cabin. Other settlers in the area also glimpsed natives in war paint scouting the western border lands, and several raiding parties attacked the settlements, bent on exacting revenge for the death of Chief Cornstalk and the other prisoners who were murdered at Fort Randolph.

In April a group of militia was ambushed while patrolling the river about five miles from Fort Culbertson, and most were killed or wounded. The Fort was also attacked, but no one was injured. Several miles away a band of forty renegades Indians descended upon the settlers at Wolf Creek, killing many of the homesteaders.

In late May, militia scouts reported to Fort Randolph that hundreds of rafts had been seen crossing the Ohio River, each one filled with Indians armed for battle.

The following day over two hundred natives from the Wyandot and Mingo tribes arrived at the gates of the stockade, demanding that the settlers surrender. Knowing that if he did so everyone in the fort would be killed, Commander McKee refused. The Indians did not immediately attack. Instead they slaughtered a herd of cattle that was grazing in a nearby field, and built fires over which to cook them.

The next morning the Indians returned and asked to be allowed entrance into the fort to make a peace treaty. Believing that their request was a ruse, the Commander instead sent Chief

Cornstalk's sister Nonhelema, who was still at the fort, outside to treat with the Indians.

Realizing that they would not be able defeat the well armed militia within the stockade, the Indians made a false peace agreement with Nonhelema, promising to return to their villages. Instead, they turned and made their way towards the unsuspecting Greenbrier settlements.

Militia scouts followed the war party to make sure they left the territory. But when the scouts returned and reported to the Commander that the Indians had split into several small groups and headed south, McKee knew that someone had to warn the frontier families that lived along the border of the approaching danger.

Gathering the militia together, McKee asked for volunteers to undertake a daring mission to alert the settlements of the coming attack. Two young men, John Pryor and Philip Hammond, immediately stepped forward.

With the help of Cornstalk's sister, the frontiersmen dressed themselves in Indian garb and donned war paint, so that if they were seen by any raiding parties they would be mistaken for braves. Waiting for the cover of darkness, the fearless men raced through the forest towards the white settlements.

When Pryor and Hammond reached the McClung homestead the next day and warned him of the large force of Indians that was only a few miles behind them, William quickly gathered his family and slipped silently into the trees. They hurried towards the fort down the path he had prepared for them, a journey of around ten miles, and arrived safely at Fort Donnally just before nightfall. Probably the only reason that the McClungs were not overtaken and killed was

105

that the Indians, upon arriving at the McClung farm, saw a large number of hogs in a pen near his cabin and stopped long enough to kill and eat them.

The fortifications at Fort Donnally consisted of a rectangular stockade made of upright posts whose ends were sharpened to a point, making it difficult for anyone to scale the walls. The stockade fence was ninety feet long and eighty feet wide. Within the fence was a single building, a large two story double log house which had an earthen cellar, a double central chimney, and large stone piers that supported the second story of the structure.

At the time of the Indian uprising there were over sixty pioneers taking shelter in the house, most of whom were women and young children. There were fewer than thirty able bodied men available to defend the fort from the rapidly approaching renegades.

Sometime during the night of May 28, the Indians arrived at a point called Bald Knob on Brushy Ridge, about one mile from the fort. They halted and spent the night on the ridge, waiting for sunrise to make a surprise attack on the settlers in the valley below.

Just before dawn, as was his custom, Colonel Donnally's aged Irish servant William Prichart opened the stockade gate. Seeing nothing unusual, he walked to the wood pile to get an armload of kindling to start the morning fires.

The war party had left Bald Knob about an hour earlier and followed the creek down to the fort. Seeing that the stockade gate was open one warrior ran out of the forest and downed Prichart with a single blow from his tomahawk, killing him instantly. The Indians rushed the fort and several managed to get through the gate and to the door of the blockhouse, which was standing ajar.

Fortunately, there were a few men just inside the door that saw the advancing savages. One of the men, William Hughart, calmly said "Yonder they come." and slammed the heavy door shut just as the first of the Indians reached the threshold.

The Indians began chopping the door with their tomahawks in an effort to pry it open. As it began to buckle inward from the weight of the attackers, a huge black man rushed forward and threw himself against the door, preventing the Indians from gaining entry into the house. Soon the alarm was sounded and the small band of frontiersmen, rifles in hand, rushed to the defense of the fort.

William McClung and several other

militiamen fired a withering volley into the natives that were already within the stockade walls, driving them back through the gate, which was quickly secured by one the settlers. The enraged Indians, angry that their surprise attack had been thwarted, advanced and began firing on the fort.

The battle raged fiercely for over ten hours, with the small group of frontiersmen holding off over two hundred braves. Many of the women in the fort, including Abigail McClung, bravely stood beside their men to help reload rifles and make bullets during the long onslaught. Most of the women were still in their night clothes since there had been no time to dress when the alarm was raised.

The Indians tried several tactics to regain entry into the fort, which included climbing nearby trees in order to shoot into the stockade and throwing burning torches onto the roof of the house. But largely due to William McClung and his prowess with the carbine long rifle he wielded, they were not successful.

When word of the battle reached Fort Savannah at Lewisburg, Colonel Lewis and Captain Stuart immediately set out with sixty men to relieve the besieged homesteaders. The men made a long march through the forest, never stopping for breaks in their hurry to relieve the small band of settlers that were trapped in the small stockade. Most of the men from Fort Savannah were relatives or friends of the homesteaders that lived along Big Clear Creek and Meadow River, and they feared that they would not reach Fort Donnally before the war party had killed or kidnaped the whites, as they had done at Muddy Creek.

When the rescue party approached the

fort they did not hear gunfire and thought that the battle was already over. However, several natives in war paint were spotted hiding among the trees, so the men made a run for the fort as the warriors opened fire. Although every man in the detachment had at least one bullet hole in his clothing when they reached the stockade, not one of the soldiers was wounded in the wild dash across the field.

Infuriated, the Indians renewed their attack, but after a short battle with the militia in the reenforced stockade, the surviving savages gave up and disappeared into the forest. At least seventeen of the raiding party had been killed during the assault, and probably more, since a large number of the wounded warriors were carried away in the retreat.

Only four of the militia men in the stockade were killed, thanks to the skill of sharpshooters like William McClung his brother Charles, who had also sought shelter at the fort. After the Indians had withdrawn, several men accused Charles of being a spy for the war party, since his friendship with the local tribes was well known. Only William's stout defense of his brother prevented the angry mob from executing him. It was later proven that Charles was innocent of the charges that were brought against him. The border men, although quick to judge, were equally quick to admit their mistake and asked for pardon from the McClung brothers.

The heroism of Captain William McClung and the other militiamen who held the fort against incredible odds soon became well known on the border. Tales of the incredible shots made by William that prevented the Indians from setting fire to the stockade soon grew into legends that were told around every pioneer hearth in Greenbrier County.

The brave actions of Dick Pointer, Colonel Donnally's slave who held the door against twenty Indians until the sleeping settlers could be roused, were also instrumental in saving the fort. Pointer later received his freedom for his part in the battle, and the grateful survivors built him a cabin and gave him a lifetime lease on the property.

The attack at Fort Donnally was one of the largest Revolutionary War battles fought in what is now West Virginia. Although the Indian attacks against the homesteaders on the western border continued for many years, none matched it in size or ferocity.

After the Indians had retreated to their villages across the Ohio River, William McClung gathered his family and headed back to his homestead, hoping that there would be no further invasions by the British and their Indian allies into Greenbrier County.

CHAPTER NINE
THE BATTLE OF COWPENS

Following the American victory at Fort Donnally, the settlers were able to remain on their homesteads and plant a summer crop. Only a few isolated attacks by roving bands of natives took place during the following months.

In 1779 there were a series of American successes against the British and Indians, headed by George Rogers Clark, who was appointed by the Virginia legislature to take an expedition to the west to route the British from the garrisons they held there. Clark and one hundred and seventy five men managed to take the British posts at Kaskaskia, Cahokia and Vincennes.

Clark's campaign was so successful that delegations from the Wyandot and Shawnee nations traveled to Fort Pitt to make terms of peace with the authorities there.

The next two years passed peacefully in the western settlements. The Americans were still embroiled in the fight for Independence, but none of the battles were fought in the Greenbrier region of Virginia.

In the spring of 1780, Abigail gave birth to a little girl. It was the couple's second daughter and sixth child, whom they named Mary. The couple doted on the baby, and it seemed for a time that life had returned to normal for the pioneer family.

William still met regularly with the local company of militia that he was attached to, but they were seldom called out for active duty. William was happy to remain at home, spending his time farming and hunting and making improvements on the homestead. But that was about to change.

All that year the rebel forces in South

116

Carolina had suffered disastrous losses at the hands of the regular British army. Desperate, George Washington appointed Nathaniel Greene as commander of the Southern Department of the Continental forces. When Greene took command of the southern army, it consisted of only fifteen hundred men. Governor Thomas Jefferson ordered that the Greenbrier militia must provide 137 men for a limited draft (three to six months). Rockbridge, Augusta, Botetort and Greenbrier counties all provided experienced men to fight with the regular army, which was in particular need of skilled marksmen.

William McClung, now in his forties, was still an excellent example of manhood, tall, slender and muscular; with an imposing appearance and the keen eyes of a shooter. McClung presented a striking figure in his buckskin hunting attire, with his six foot long flintlock rifle slung across his shoulder. He readily agreed to take part in the draft, and was placed in Captain James Gilmore's Rockbridge County Company. Gilmore's troops were often referred to as the 'Rockbridge Rifles' because all of the men in the regiment owned their own guns (unlike the other divisions who had to be issued weapons) and were unparalleled marksmen.

The Rockbridge Rifles were ordered to join Greene's division, so in the fall of 1780 the company made the one hundred mile march to South Carolina.

Nathaniel Greene's second in command was Brigade General Daniel Morgan, an experienced soldier who had fought in the French and Indian War and at the Siege of Boston. Greene divided the invigorated forces into two divisions, with himself at the head of one and Morgan at the head of the other.

Morgans's troops contained several companies of militia, including those commanded by Major Frank Triplett, Captain James Tate and Captain James Gilmore.

Morgan's army was ordered to march west to the Catawba River, and join with the forces of Andrew Pickens. On December 21 Morgan set out with six hundred men, four hundred of which were regular troops, the rest being militiamen from Virginia.

Lord Cornwallis, the commander of the British regular army, was traveling from South Carolina to North Carolina when his scouts reported that Morgan was leading a large army into the state and would soon intersect with the left division of the English troops.

Cornwallis gave orders to one of his Lieutenant Colonels, Banastre Tarlton, to take a division and cut off the patriot army. Tarleton had a reputation for being a skilled but ruthless commander and was hated by the Americans because after winning a victory at the Battle of Warsaw, he ordered his troops to kill all the colonial soldiers, even though they had already laid down their arms and surrendered.

Tarleton marched his troops to a clearing where he believed he would encounter the rebel army, but they were not there. Infuriated, instead of returning to the main army and reporting to Lord Cornwallis, he decided to pursue the Americans. Tarleton sent a post to Cornwallis informing him of his plans and asking for additional troops, which Cornwallis supplied.

When Morgan learned from his scouts that a division of British soldiers was in pursuit and that another force under Cornwallis was approaching from his right, he retreated north in order to avoid being trapped between the two armies.

On the fifteenth of January, Morgan and his men reached the swollen banks of the Broad River. Not wishing to be attacked while trying to cross the flooding water, Morgan decided to stand and fight the oncoming British. He led his army to a nearby pasture that was often used for grazing cattle. The rolling landscape had unique properties that Morgan included in his strategy for the upcoming battle.

Morgan choose a small hill in the middle of the pasture to be the center of his position. There he placed his Continental Infantrymen. He deliberately left his flanks open, believing (correctly) that Tarlton would attack his troops head on.

Morgan then set up three lines of soldiers. The first line was made up of one hundred and fifty regular army shooters (skirmishers), the second of three hundred sharpshooters from the militia, and the third of five hundred and fifty experienced regulars.

The first line of skirmishers were given orders to fire at will into the advancing British until the army reached the base of the hill, then make an orderly retreat to the rear. The three hundred militia men were instructed to fire two volleys into the oncoming troops and then to withdraw to the left and reform behind the regulars. This movement of the militia in the second line would mask the third line from the British troops.

Morgan's tactical goal was to weaken and disorganize Tarleton's forces, who would have to march uphill to engage the Americans. Because the British troops would already be suffering physical and psychological damage by the time they reached the third line of regulars, it would give the American troops a decided advantage in the battle.

The topography had provided a large ravine on the right of the pasture, and a creek on the left, protecting the soldiers from any flanking movements that Tarleton attempted. Morgan assured his men that "The whole idea is to lead Tarleton into a trap so we can beat his cavalry and infantry as they come up those slopes. When they've been cut down to size by our fire, we'll attack them."

William McClung took his position in the second line on the hill with the other militiamen from the Rockbridge Rifles unit. Several of the younger frontiersmen had never fought in a regular army battle and were unsettled, but McClung and the other 'old heads' kept up a light banter and tried to put their companions at ease. The militia loaded their weapons, waiting for the encroaching army to make an appearance at the edge of the surrounding forest.

In his desire to overtake Morgan before he could cross the Broad River and escape, Tarelton had pushed his troops mercilessly for five days, never stopping long enough for them to get adequate food or rest. In the final forty eight hours before reaching Cowpens, the army ran out of food and had less that four hours of sleep. As a result, the men were exhausted when they finally met the opposing forces.

Tarleton's strategy for the battle was simple. His scouts had informed him of the layout of Morgan's troops on the small hill, with a ravine on one side and a creek on the other.

Believing Morgan's tactics were flawed, he ordered his infantry into linear formation and had them move directly up the hill towards the opposing army. His right and left flanks were protected by dragoons (cavalry) and he positioned his two grasshopper cannons in the center of his infantry. Tarleton kept two hundred cavalry in reserve to be used when the Americans tried to break and run.

Tarleton gave his troops the order to advance, and his infantry stormed the hill. His men, dressed in bright green uniforms that made them easy targets, marched forward in the accepted military fashion, only to be met by a sharp volley of gunfire from the first line of skirmishers.

Next Tarleton sent in his cavalry, ordering them to attack the opposing forces. The rebel army shot in unison, and fifteen riders were hit and dropped from their mounts. The remainder retreated. In a fury, Tarleton ordered his infantrymen to charge and take the hill, without waiting for the rest of his army to

125

advance onto the field of battle.

The infantry started up the embankment, taking the two cannons with them. The skirmishers fired again, then melted back into the line of militia men waiting in the vanguard.

William McClung and the frontiersmen stepped forward within range of the advancing British infantry and fired two deadly volleys, just as they had been ordered to do. Almost half of the shots hit British officers, leaving the English troops both astonished and confused, since soldiers in the regular army rarely targeted enemy commanders during a battle. The militia then turned in an orderly fashion and moved to the rear as they had been commanded.

Thinking that the American forces were in full retreat, Tarleton commanded his men to rush the opposing line. They did so, but in an unorganized chaos that left them open to attack.

Seizing the opportunity, the militia commander shouted to his men to return to the battle and fire on the approaching infantry. William McClung and his comrades turned cooly and shot a volley with deadly accuracy into the disoriented troops who were no more than thirty yards away. Dozens of men fell, dead before they hit the ground. The British infantrymen staggered, slowed by their fallen companions, but still pushed forward.

Realizing his men would not have time to reload before the enemy would be on them, the commander yelled "Charge bayonets!" The militiamen locked their bayonets and rushed headlong into the melee. The hardy frontiersmen were unequaled when it came to hand to hand combat, and the English soldiers fell by the dozens.

Tarelton's soldiers were completely

outmatched and began to collapse onto the ground, even those who were not injured. Many of the troops surrendered on the spot, while the rest turned and ran.

Tarleton ordered his cavalry to charge, but they refused and retreated from the field. Desperate, Tarleton enlisted the few remaining dragoons to ride back with him and retrieve his cannons, which had been captured by the frontiersmen. However, at the sight of William McClung and the Rockbridge Riflemen, clad in their buckskins and fur hats, with their deadly carbine rifles aimed directly at him, Tarleton turned his horse and fled.

As he rode from the battlefield several American officers fired at Tarleton, but he was not hit. He returned fire and managed to shoot a horse that one of the rebel commanders sat on, and then escaped into the woods.

The battle of Cowpens (made famous in the Mel Gibson movie "The Patriot") was a surprise victory for the colonial army. It was a major turning point in the Revolutionary War, and was instrumental in releasing South Carolina from British control. The American success against Cornwallis' forces reinvigorated the patriots, and at the same time demoralized the British and the loyalists.

The Rockbridge Rifles did not participate in any other major battles during their three month enlistment, and in the spring of 1781 William McClung made the long journey back to his home on Big Clear Creek.

Sporadic Indian raids continued along the Greenbrier border, forcing the settlers to stay ready for unexpected attacks. Even after Cornwallis surrendered the British army at Yorktown, the English continued to encourage the Indians to harass the frontier settlements.

On the McClung homestead, where the family had welcomed their seventh child, Charles, William instructed everyone to stay close to the cabin, and he did not venture out unless he had a loaded gun. The older boys, John and James, were rapidly becoming young men and shared the responsibility of guarding the homestead.

It was not until the winter of 1782 that the British government finally halted the Indian warfare along the Virginia frontier, when they directed their commander Sir Guy Carlton to order the officers at the English garrisons in the west to stop the attacks on the settlers.

After ten years of war with the British and the western Indian tribes, the border settlers had peace at last.

CHAPTER TEN
GRANDFATHER BILLIE

By the spring of 1783, the long suffering homesteaders along the Virginia frontier began to feel safe and secure from any further Indian uprisings. The end of the war brought many changes to Greenbrier County. Lands that had previously been unavailable were opened up to Americans wanting to push westward, and the isolated forests were being settled. New roads were built that could accommodate wagons and stage coaches, and small villages became thriving towns.

The family of William and Abigail McClung continued to prosper and grow. In 1784 the couple welcomed their eighth child, a boy named Samuel. Two years later they had a daughter that they called Abigail Dickenson McClung, after Abigail's mother. In 1788 a

131

daughter Janet was born, and Abigail gave birth to their eleventh and final child in 1792, a son named Alexander.

Even though several rooms had been added to the pioneer cabin over the years, William realized that his growing family needed a much larger place to live. He built their third and final house at the top of a hill about two hundred yards away from his second cabin. Although constructed of logs, the structure was a real house, two stories tall, with solid puncheon floors and real glass panes in all of its numerous windows.

William's two oldest sons, who were now nearing adulthood, did much of the work involved in building the new house, although their father was still a strong and able man, even in his fifties. The entire first floor was taken up by a combination kitchen and living area that must have seemed spacious after a lifetime of one and two room cabins. Along the front of the house the men added a long covered porch with a set of wide steps. William and Abigail loved to rest in the shade of the porch and watch their children at play. The McClung place, as it was called, was the largest and nicest home in the Meadow Bluff settlement for many years. It became the focal point for many of the social, religious and political gatherings in the area. The first elections ever held in the Meadow Bluff district took place in William and Abigail's house.

William had become one of the most prosperous men in the county. In addition to the tomahawk entry he had taken years before, he had been awarded one hundred acres of land by the new American government for his service during the Revolutionary War. He also entered a claim for two hundred and thirty acres on Slab Camp Creek, and after the war became a partner in a land enterprise with Andrew Welsh and his brother-in-law Andrew Moore. Together, they patented forty three thousand acres of land in Nicholas County.

William was happy to see the border lands becoming settled. He and Abigail had always wanted their children to have a proper education, but there were no schools on the western end of the county. William agreed to donate an old blockhouse that stood on his property to be used as a schoolhouse for the local children if a suitable teacher could be found.

It was arranged for Colonel Arbuckle, an instructor from Augusta, Virginia to move to Greenbrier County and teach at the little school located at the mouth of Little Clear Creek. In

1793 the wooden blockhouse opened its doors to fifteen young men (girls could not attend), making it the first official school in the Meadow Bluff district.

William was equally generous to the religious community. His family had always been devoted Presbyterians, and had left Scotland to be able to worship as they chose. When the local Presbyterian congregation grew large enough to support a church building and cemetery, William gladly donated two acres of land just east of Rupert for that purpose. A small Presbyterian church was built on the property, which later changed hands and is now home to the Amwell Baptist Church near the town of Rupert, WV.

In 1796 the Presbyterians erected a large stone church in Lewisburg, about twenty miles from the McClung homestead. Although the building was christened The Old Stone Presbyterian Church, to area residents it was known simply as 'The Old Stone Church'.

William often made the long trip on horseback to attend Sunday services at the church. He eventually was chosen as one of the Elders of the congregation, which was a position of authority in the community.

The McClung's eleven children became adults and began to marry. They all had large families of their own, and with so many grandchildren living near the old homestead, William eventually became known to everyone in the area as 'Grandfather Billie'.

William often boasted that he could stand in the doorway of his house, blow his bugle and call two hundred of his descendants to breakfast. Legend says that he actually did that very thing on more than one occasion.

As the family grew, William was known to give one hundred acre tracts of land to his children as wedding gifts or when they presented him with a new grandchild.

Most of the William's children settled in West Virginia. His oldest son John lived within a mile of the town of Rupert, WV. He ran a blacksmith shop and was known as 'Black John'. John was well known for his strength and his love of hunting. He married Jane Bollar in 1793, and eventually became the post master in Rupert. He and Jane had ten children. When Jane died in 1828, John married Hannah McMillion, and they had five children.

James McClung and William (Chunky Billie) settled in the Meadow Bluff district and married sisters, Mary Alderson and Jane Alderson. James and Mary had nine children. Billie and his wife Jane had ten children.

Catherine McClung married Jonas McCutcheon in 1799, and the couple lived in Greenbrier County for many years, and are believed to have had four children.

Joseph McClung, who was called Cranberry Joe, settled in the Mt. Lookout area. He was married twice, to Jane Cavendish who died at the age of 49 in 1828, with whom he had seven children. Later he married Hester Amick with whom he had two more sons.

Mary wed James McCutcheon in 1799, and the couple made their home near Rupert and had six children.

Charles McClung married Charity Vandel in 1805. They lived in Greenbrier County for several years before moving to Nicholas County. Their son Charles was a well known bricklayer in the area.

Samuel McClung married Sarah Hinton

on April 16, 1804. They lived in Greenbrier
County and had ten children.

Abigail Dickenson Mcclung married
Joseph Black in 1804. One of their descendants
was Samuel Black, a well known minister. The
Sam Black Memorial Church near Meadow
Bluff was named in his honor and is still in use
today. It sits just off the 164 interstate exit in
WV.

Janet, William and Abigail's youngest
daughter, married Andrew Cavendish in 1809.
Her husband was related to Lord Cavendish, a
prominent nobleman in England. They lived in
Meadow bluff and had a large family.

The McClung's youngest son Alexander,
called Stumpy Alex, married Rebecca Cavendish
in 1816. They lived in Greenbrier County and
had twelve children.

William's beloved wife Abigail died at

the couple's two story log house in Meadow Bluff on November 7, 1820. She was seventy-four years old.

Although he never fully recovered from her loss, William continued to live in his home and farm his land for the next thirteen years, remaining a strong and active member of the community until his death.

William McClung lived a life that few people even dream of. He was a pioneer, a frontiersman, an Indian fighter and a soldier in the Revolutionary War. He was a husband, a father, a farmer, a loyal friend and an honorable man.

Much like adventurers Daniel Boone and Davy Crockett, William McClung was a true American hero. He died on January 18, 1833 at the venerable age of ninety-five, and was buried beside Abigail at the Otter Creek Cemetery (the

Old Amwell Cemetery) in Greenbrier County.

The inscription on his headstone reads:

William McClung

Virginia

Ensign

Va. Militia

Revolutionary War

1738 - 1833

Bibliography

McClung, Reba Irene. *The Greenbrier McClung Way*. Parkersburg, WV., Easton Printing Co.1990.

Rice, Otis K., *A History of Greenbrier County*. Parsons, WV, McCain Printing Co., 1986.

Dayton, Ruth Woods., *Greenbrier Pioneers and Their Homes*., Charleston, WV., West Virginia Publishing Company. 1942.

Hale, John P., *Trans-Allegheny Pioneers*., Raleigh, N.C., Derreth Printing Company., 1971.

Richmond, Nancy., *Ghosts of Greenbrier County*, Charleston, SC.,CreateSpace Publishing,. 2010

Richmond, Nancy., *Appalachian Folklore: Omens, Signs and Superstitions*., Charleston, SC., CreateSpace Publishing, 2011

http://rockbrdigeadvocate.com/odell/cowpens.htm

http://www.wvculture.org/history/settlement/fortdonnally04.html

http://www.wvencyclopedia.org/articles/2375

http://www.meadowbluff.com/greenbrier/1221.html

http://en.wikipedia.org/wiki/Battle_of_Cowpens

Made in the USA
Middletown, DE
15 November 2017